DORSET IN PHOTOGRAPHS

MATTHEW PINNER

AMBERLEY

First published 2017

Amberley Publishing
The Hill, Stroud
Gloucestershire, GL5 4EP

www.amberley-books.com

Copyright © Matthew Pinner, 2017

The right of Matthew Pinner to be identified as the Author of this work has been
asserted in accordance with the Copyrights, Designs and Patents Act 1988.

ISBN 978 1 4456 7692 0 (print)
ISBN 978 1 4456 7693 7 (ebook)

British Library Cataloguing in Publication Data.
A catalogue record for this book is available from the British Library.

Origination by Amberley Publishing.
Printed in the UK.

ABOUT THE PHOTOGRAPHER

Matthew Pinner is a Dorset landscape photographer who is based within the town of Christchurch. He bought his first camera after his grandfather sadly passed away and left him his tripod in his will.

The main driving factor behind the making of this book has been the overwhelming support from Matthew's vast social following – 150,000 across all media platforms. He has achieved a fair bit of success already within his career, having provided many of his images to notable networks such as the BBC, ITV and major national newspapers. Leading companies within the photography world have also taken an interest in his work, supporting him through social media channels. Matthew uses a Canon 5D Mark 3, along with Canon lenses and Lee Filters.

Website: pinners-photography.co.uk
Facebook: Pinners Photography
Twitter: Matt_Pinner
Instagram: Matt_Pinner
Email: enquiriespinnersphotography.co.uk

ACKNOWLEDGEMENTS

I would like to thank several people that have helped me along the way, not only with this book but with my photography in general. Firstly, my fiancée Emma for sticking by me through all the early mornings to get that perfect sunrise, and all the late sunsets. It must be true love if you agreed to marry me after all I ask of you in aid of my career. Also, my family: my mum, dad, brother and sister, thank you for supporting me through all of the ups and downs I have faced within this industry. My long-term friend Dave, who took me out most days when I gained my interest in photography all those years ago. If it weren't for you, I wouldn't have discovered so many fantastic locations to photograph.

There has also been some amazing support from individuals that have been within the photography world for a while and I would love to give them praise for this achievement: Canon UK & Ireland, Angela Nicholson, Simon Parkin from *ITV Weather*, Helen Stiles from *Dorset Magazine*, Dorset Tourism, Caroline Sharp from Lulworth Estates, John Challis, Jade Grassby from *Bournemouth Echo*, Dean Murray from Cover Images, BBC Earth, Elliot Wagland, Paul Vass from BNPS, Rosie Barratt from *Amateur Photography Magazine*, and Robbie-Lee Valentine.

Lastly, I would like to thank all the photographers who have inspired me and kept me pushing the limits of my work:

Kevin Ferrioli (www.facebook.com/k.ferrioli)
Nick Lucas (www.facebook.com/nick.lucas.1614)
Martin Dolan (www.facebook.com/martindolanphotography)
Paul Dimarco (www.facebook.com/paul.dimarco.16)
Zoe Davis (www.facebook.com/zoedavisphotography1992)
Mark Bauer (www.facebook.com/MarkBauerPhotography)

INTRODUCTION

I first became interested in photography after I was given my first tripod; let's just say the rest is history. I live by the saying that you miss every shot you don't take. When I have a spare moment, I will be off researching the next place to capture with my camera, and when I'm free to explore I'm off roaming around Dorset and the Jurassic Coast.

SPRING

Barn, Sixpenny Handley

Corfe Castle

Bluebell field, near Shaftesbury

West Bay

Sandbags, near Mudeford

Christchurch Quay

Portland Bill Lighthouse

Colmer's Hill, near Bridport

Farmer's field, near Ringstead

Knowlton Church

View from Maiden Castle

Old Harry Rocks

Highcliffe Castle

Kimmeridge Bay

St Aldhelm's Chapel, near Swanage

Wild garlic field,
near Kimmeridge

Wimborne Minster

Badbury Rings

Sandbanks

Corfe Village

Gold Hill

Pulpit Rock, Portland Bill

Durdle Door

Blue Pool, near Arne

Sandbanks

White Mill, near Wimborne

Worth Matravers

Mupe Bay

Rocky Beach, near Durdle Door

St Catherine's Church, Abbotsbury

Stanpit Marsh, near Christchurch

Kimmeridge Valley

Swanage

Coastguard station, Hengistbury Head

Horton Tower

Corfe Village

SUMMER

Mudeford Quay

River Avon, Christchurch

Durdle Door

West Bay

Wareham River

Sandbanks

Christchurch Quay

Old Harry Rocks

Hinton, near Highcliffe

Hengistbury Head

Lulworth Cove

Colmer's Hill, near Bridport

Hardy's Monument

Christchurch Priory

Fisherman's Bank, near Mudeford

Avon Beach, near Mudeford

Boscombe Pier

Sandbanks

Poppy field, near Blandford Forum

View from Colmer's Hill, near Bridport

Swanage Pier

River Avon, Christchurch

Poppy field, near Blandford Forum

Beach huts, Mudeford Spit

Mudeford Spit

Colmer's Hill, near Bridport

Badbury Rings

Bournemouth Pier

Milton Abbas

Fisherman's Walk Bay, near Mudeford

Studland

Water mill, Throop

Poppy field, near Blandford Forum

AUTUMN

Boscombe Pier

Poole Park

Littlebredy waterfall, near West Bay

Christchurch Quay

Lulworth Cove

Knowlton Church

Old Swanage Pier

Corfe Castle

White Mill, near Wimborne

Knowlton Church

Old Harry Rocks

Mammatus clouds, Mudeford Quay

Avon Beach, near Mudeford

St Catherine's Hill, near Christchurch

Lyme Regis

Misty field, near Wareham and Arne

Eyebridge, near Wimborne

Poole Park

Kimmeridge Bay

Swanage Pier

Mammatus clouds, Mudeford Pier

Portland Bill Lighthouse

Mudeford Quay

Pulpit Rock, Portland Bill

Gangway, Mudeford Spit

Steps, Blue Pool

Hengistbury Head

Fireworks, Boscombe Pier

Badbury Rings

WINTER

Sturminster Newton

Avon Beach, near Mudeford

Broken bridge, Blandford

Horton Tower

St Aldhelm's Chapel, near Swanage

Getty, Hamworthy

Man of War Bay, near Durdle Door

Durdle Door

Corfe Castle

Misty field, near Lulworth Cove

Corfe Castle

Sandbanks

Beach huts, Avon Beach

Knowlton Church

Kimmeridge Bay

Portland Bill

Mudeford Quay

Mupe Bay

Corfe Castle

Kimmeridge Bay

Durdle Door

Beach huts, Mudeford Spit

River Wareham